VINTAGE

HAND EMBROIDERY PATTERNS

KITTENS AND PUPPIES

24 Authentic Vintage Designs

Vintage Hand Embroidery Patterns

VOLUME 1

Vicki Becker

Visit my author page
http://amazon.com/author/vickibecker
to see all my needlework books

ISBN-13: 978-1546515685

ISBN-10: 1546515682

First Printing, 2017
Printed in the United States of America

Contents

About the Author.. 4

Introduction 5

How to Use the Designs...................................... 7

Transfer Methods.. 9

Embroidery Basics... 10

Embroidery Stitches... 13

Rag Quilt Throw.. 15

Envelope Pillow Cover 19

Patchwork Pillow Cover.................................... 21

The Designs 23

Envelope Pillow Cover Designs.......................... 25

Kitten and Puppy Designs................................. 29

About the Author

Vicki Becker is an avid needlework enthusiast who loves everything arts and crafts! Mrs. Becker has been knitting and crocheting for over 48 years. She learned to crochet from her grandmother in the beautiful Adirondack Mountains of upstate New York where she grew up.

Mrs. Becker shares her knowledge and experience through her books with patterns for crochet, knitting, hand embroidery, and quilting. Vicki also enjoys making puzzle books, journals, and coloring books. She creates digital art, illustrations, and mixed media art for the designs in her books.

Vicki Becker lives in central Florida with her husband, four cats, and two dogs. Her hobbies include all forms of needlework, photography, digital art, cooking, and gardening.

Vicki offers needlework tutorials and often publishes free patterns on her website http://vickisdesigns.com

Sample puzzles and coloring pages are free to download on her website http://vickibecker.com

Introduction

Vintage Kittens and Puppies hand Embroidery Patterns is the first book in this exciting series of vintage hand embroidery patterns. There are 24 authentic vintage designs in three sizes and complete instructions for making a throw size rag quilt, envelope pillow covers, and patchwork pillow covers. Instructions for transferring the designs to fabric, color tinting, and embroidery are also in the book.

Crayon tinted and embroidered designs were very popular in America from the 1920's until the mid 1950's. Iron-on transfers were used, colored with crayons, heat set, and then hand embroidered. Homemakers made household items such as table linens, pillows, dish towels, and quilts.

This book explains how to transfer the designs onto fabric, color tint, and then embroider or highlight the designs with ink. Embroidery is a great way to add a special touch to your sewing projects requiring only a few basic inexpensive tools and materials that you can find in any craft store. All you really need to get started is a needle, floss, embroidery hoop, and fabric. Crafters of all skill levels find embroidery one of the easiest and most addictive ways to personalize everyday objects.

Using the designs for hand embroidery is easy! The designs are printed on one side of a page so you can easily trace the designs or carefully remove the pages to use with a light box. You can enlarge or reduce the designs to fit your projects as needed. Use them for sewing, quilting, or embellish ready made items such as t-shirts, tote bags, aprons, and much more.

I hope you will enjoy using the designs to create something unique and beautiful for yourself or as a gift for someone special.

VINTAGE

HAND EMBROIDERY

PATTERNS

How to Use the Designs

Fabrics

100% cotton works the best for crayon tinting and embroidery. Quilter's cotton, unbleached muslin, or broadcloth is a good choice. Tone on tone fabrics look especially nice when combined with embroidery. Ready made items can include t-shirts, aprons, dish towels, tote bags, and plain pillow covers.

Pre-wash the fabric you are coloring.

Wash the fabric or item as you normally would but do not use fabric softeners. Iron the fabric so it will be smooth and free of wrinkles.

Using the designs from the book.

Scan and print, trace directly from the book, or carefully remove the page to trace with a light box. Reduce or enlarge the design if needed to fit your project. The design should be at least one inch smaller than the fabric or area you plan to embroider. Transfer the design to fabric using one of the methods explained in the transfer methods section of the book.

Stabilize the Fabric before Color Tinting

To stabilize the fabric for ease of applying color it is recommended that the fabric either be backed with contact paper or ironed onto freezer paper before coloring. To apply freezer paper to the back of your fabric place the shiny side of the paper down and iron in place. Remove the paper after coloring.

Coloring

Make sure your fabric is free of threads and lint before starting to color. I run a lint roller over the design area before I begin. Use regular or fabric crayons to color your design. When coloring, work from the top down. Crayons can smudge if you rub your hand over them while coloring. If any crayon flakes appear on your fabric, don't wipe them away, instead gently blow them from the fabric to prevent smudging. In applying crayons, use the method you like best just so the fabric will be completely colored. I like to use a small circular motion. For deep, rich effects, apply the crayon heavily. Rub one color over another for mixtures. A color over white crayon produces a tint.

Heat Setting the Design

Use white paper towels or plain paper to heat set the design. The iron needs to be set to the hottest temperature that the fabric used can withstand with no steam. Remove the freezer or contact paper from the back of the fabric and place design face up on paper towels or paper to protect your ironing board. Cover the design area with a layer of white paper towels or paper to absorb the excess wax and begin pressing. Change the paper and continue pressing until there is no longer any wax color coming off on the paper. When you are finished, turn the fabric over and steam set the backside of your crayoned design. The colors of the design will be lighter after heat setting. If you are not pleased with the results you can go back and repeat the coloring and heat setting process again.

Ink or Embroider the Design

To finish your design use Pigma Micron permanent ink pens or Pentel gel rollers for fabric to outline and highlight the design. You can also embroider the design. You will find tips for embroidery in the embroidery section of the book.

Fabric Care

When washing your completed item, do not use harsh detergents, wash in cold water and dry on a low heat setting or air dry.

Transfer Methods

Light Method

The method I use most to trace the designs is by using a light box or window. This method is used for light colored fabrics and items that when a light is behind the paper pattern and fabric you can see the lines to trace the design onto the fabric.

When tracing the designs to fabric use masking tape or pins to secure the paper pattern onto the wrong side so it doesn't move. You can then move the fabric around on the light box when tracing. Trace the design using a Pigma Micron pen or any permanent ink pen. I don't use markers because they smudge and spread into the fabric making the lines too thick.

If you don't have a light box you can use things you may have around the house or just use a window. I've used my sliding glass door on a sunny afternoon. I've also used a glass coffee table with a light underneath and a glass cutting board held up by cups and a small flat LED flashlight underneath.

You can purchase inexpensive light boxes or even build your own. My husband built me a nice light box from scrap plywood. I had a piece of Plexiglas cut to size at the hardware store and then placed a small fluorescent light strip I found at IKEA inside the box. Use a cool light source such as fluorescent or LED.

Transfer Pen or Pencil Method

This method is used for fabrics and items that you can't easily see through when a light source is placed behind it. I use this method for darker color t-shirts, canvas tote bags, aprons, and light weight chambray or denim. To trace the designs you will need a hot-iron transfer pen or pencil. Sulky brand transfer pens come in a variety of colors, including white for use on dark colored fabrics.

Trace the design with the transfer pen or pencil by placing the paper on a light box or window print side down. Trace the design on the back side of the paper pattern. You can also use tracing paper placed on top of the design to trace. If you use this method make sure to make a mirror image of the design first if direction is important as in monograms and lettering.

Pin the design to the fabric and iron the design to your fabric following the directions for the pen or pencils you are using. Cover the design with a piece of plain paper to protect your iron and use the hottest setting usually the cotton setting. Press, then lift the iron and press another area until your design is transferred. Do not rub the iron around on the paper as the design may shift and cause the lines to be blurry. You can check to see if the image has transferred by removing a pin and lifting a corner of the paper.

Embroidery Basics

Hand Embroidery

Hand embroidery has a lot in common with the relaxation qualities of coloring. Embroidery is an art form that has brought pleasure and admiration for centuries. There really can be no mistakes as each creation is your own personal art production. Your selections of yarns, threads, colors and techniques makes each embroidered creation uniquely yours.

Supplies

Embroidery requires only a few basic inexpensive tools and materials that you can find in any craft store. All you really need to get started is a needle, floss, and some fabric but there are a few other items that will come in handy as well.

Embroidery Floss

Embroidery floss comes in many colors and is sold in small bundles or skeins. Floss is made up of six threads or plies twisted together. To embroider measure off and cut twelve to eighteen inches of floss and separate the threads into groups to stitch with. Most embroidery projects are stitched using two or three plys together but you can use up to six.

Embroidery Hoops

Embroidery hoops have two round frames that fit together and tighten with a screw. The frames hold your fabric tightly between them as you stitch. They come in plastic or wood and in many different sizes. You can use different sized hoops for different sized projects, but I've found that an 6 inch circle is a good one for most projects.

Hooping your fabric will give you a tight, smooth surface to stitch on, and will prevent puckering. To hoop your fabric, first loosen the screw and separte the two parts of the hoop. The section of the embroidery to be worked is place over the smaller of the hoops. The larger hoop is then pressed down over the fabric onto the smaller hoop. The last step is to tighten the screw to hold the work taut.

Needles

There's really no special size or type of needle you have to use for embroidering. All you really need is one with a sharp point and an eye large enough for you to thread easily. You might also want a small pincushion close by so your needles don't get lost.

Fabric Stabilizer

You may want to apply a fabric stabilizer to the back of your project before embroidering to keep the fabric from stretching while you work. Stretchy, flimsy, and loose weave fabrics are much easier to embroider if you first apply a fabric stabilizer to the back. There are many types of fabric stabilizer. Look for a thinner, iron-on stabilizer intended for machine embroidery because it's easier to stitch through.

To apply the stabilizer, cut a piece slightly larger than the entire design. Iron the fabric to remove wrinkles and apply the stabilizer to the back of the fabric, or wrong side, according to the instructions on the package. After you finish embroidering the entire design, you can remove the stabilizer by carefully pulling it from the fabric. Then use tweezers to remove any bits of stabilizer that may be caught under the stitches.

Scissors

Keep a pair of small sharp sewing scissors on hand while embroidering. You need them to cut lengths of floss and snip off any leftover floss when you're finished stitching. Embroidery scissors are 4 to 5 inches long and have very sharp points.

Needle Threader

If you are having trouble threading your needle a needle threader makes the job quick and easy.

VINTAGE

HAND EMBROIDERY

PATTERNS

Embroidery Stitches

Although there are over 300 named embroidery stitches, only a few stitches generally are used for tinted embroidery. The outline stitch or stem stitch is often used, as the name implies to create flower stems or to outline pictures. The straight stitch may be used for highlighting or for parallel short lines as in the fur on a rabbit. The satin stitch is often used for filing in. The French knot is frequently used for dots, as in flower centers or for small eyes as in an animal. The loop stitch or lazy daisy stitch is often used for flower petals or leaves. Any of these stitches, or a combination of them, may go into a single piece to achieve the effects you want.

Stitching the Design

Start stitching by leaving a 3-4 inch length of floss on the back side of the work to be woven in later. No knots should appear on the wrong side of the work. When the thread becomes too short finish it off by drawing the thread to the wrong side of the work. Weave the needle in and out of the stitches of the completed embroidery, then cut the thread close to the work. The wrong side of the work should be as neat as the right side, therefore do not carry the thread from one design area to another.

Outline or Stem Stitch

This stitch is worked from left to right, taking regular, slightly slanting stitches along the line of the design. The thread always emerges on the left side of the previous stitch. This stitch is used for flower stems and outlines.

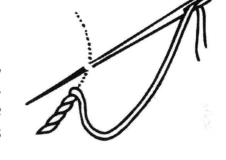

Straight Stitch

This is shown as single, spaced stitches worked either in a regular or irregular manner. Sometimes the stitches are of varying size. The stitches should be neither too long nor too loose.

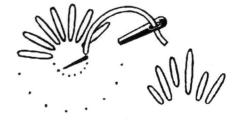

Cross Stitch

Bring the needle through on the lower right line of the cross and insert at the top of the same line, taking a stitch through the fabric to lower left line (A). Continue to the end of the row in this way and on the return journey, complete the other half of the cross (B). It is important that the top strands of all the stitches point in one direction.

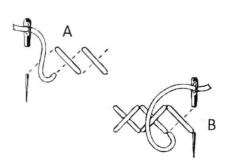

Back Stitch

Bring the thread through on the stitching line, and then take a small backward stitch through the fabric. Bring the needle through again a little in front of the first stitch, take another backward stitch, pushing the needle in at the point where it first came through.

Satin Stitch

Work Straight Stitches across the shape as shown in the diagram. If desired, Running Stitch or Back Stitch may be worked first to form padding underneath, to give a raised effect. Care must be taken to keep a good edge. Do not make the stitches too long, as then they could be pulled out of position.

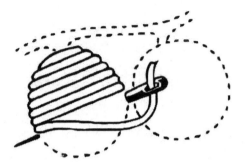

Long and Short Stitch

This form of Satin Stitch is so named as all the stitches are of varying lengths. It is often used to fill a shape which is too large or too irregular to be covered by Satin Stitch and it also can be used to achieve a shaded effect.

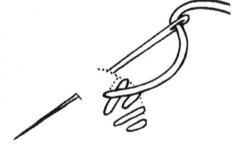

Lazy Daisy Stitch

Bring the thread out at the top of the line and hold own with your left thumb. Insert the needle where it last emerged and bring the point out a short distance away (A). Fasten each loop at the foot with a small stitch (B). This stitch may be worked singly or in groups to form flower petals.

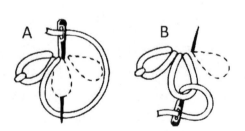

French Knots

Bring the thread out at the required position. Hold the thread down with the left thumb and encircle the thread twice with the needle (1). Still holding the thread firmly, twist the needle back to the starting point and insert it close to where the thread first emerged (2). Pull thread through to the back and secure to finish making the French knot (3).

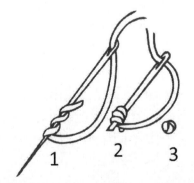

Rag Quilt Throw

Rag quilts are so quick and easy to make that once you learn how to make them; you won't be able to stop! The quilts are made using a quilt-as-you-go method, meaning that each piece of fabric is sandwiched with its batting and backing before the quilt is stitched together. The technique that makes rag quilting unique from other quilting methods is the fraying of exposed seams. This gives rag quilts their characteristic "raggedy" appearance. Use any embroidery design you wish on the design squares.

Project Specifications

Skill Level: Beginner

Finished Quilt Size: 47.5 X 57 inches

Block Size: 9 ½" X 9 ½"

Number of Blocks: 30

Yardage Requirements

Note: Yardage is based on 45" wide fabric. Quilt batting is based on 90" batting sold by the yard.

Fabric & Batting

1 ½ yd - Unbleached muslin, broadcloth, or quilter's cotton (cream, ivory, or white) for design squares

4 ½ yd - Assorted cotton prints in colors of your choice

7/8 yd - Low loft quilt batting

Fusible embroidery stabilizer (optional)

Supplies & Tools

Water soluble marking pen or pencil

05 (45 mm) Pigma permanent marking pen, Sulky transfer pen, or iron-on pencil

Contact or Freezer paper

Crayons

Embroidery floss (optional)

Straight pins

Sewing thread

Rotary cutter, mat, and quilting ruler

9 ½" and 10 ½" inch square quilt template rulers (optional)

6 ½" and 10 ½" inch angle quilt template rulers (optional)

Sewing machine and walking foot

Iron and ironing board

Fiskars Rag Quilt snips or any sharp scissors

6 inch embroidery hoop (optional)

Light box (optional)

Instructions

Preparing the fabric

1. Wash, dry, and iron all the fabric you will be using for the quilt. Remember not to use fabric softener for the squares that you will be coloring.

Cutting

Note: I use a 9 ½" and a 10 ½" quilt template ruler and rotary cutter to cut my squares.

1. Cut fifteen 10½" squares from unbleached muslin, broadcloth or quilters cotton for the design blocks.

2. Cut forty-five 10½" squares from assorted cotton prints for the alternate quilt blocks and backing blocks.

3. Cut thirty 9½" squares from quilt batting.

4. Cut fifteen 10½" squares from stabilizer (optional)

Preparing the design squares

1. Transfer the embroidery designs of your choice to the design squares. Color each square and then heat set. Outline and highlight each design with ink or embroidery. I used 4 plies of embroidery floss to cover the 05 (45 mm) Pigma pen lines. Refer to the book section for transferring the designs, coloring, and embroidery for more information.

Quilting

1. Lay a 10½" cotton print backing square on your ironing board wrong side up. Place a 9 ½" batting square on top, centering it ½" in from each side of the fabric. Place a 10½" cotton print or design square on top right side up, and pin the three layers together to form a quilt sandwich.

2. Mark the quilting lines with a water soluble pen or pencil. For the design blocks draw a diagonal line using the 6½" angle quilting ruler across each corner of the block measuring 2½" in from the edges and ½" in from each side.

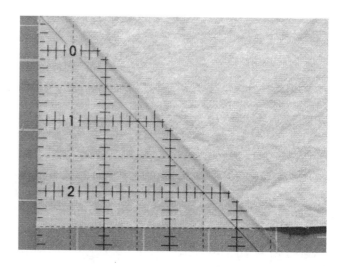

3. For the cotton print blocks draw an X across the block ½" inch from each point using the 10½" angle quilting ruler as a guide.

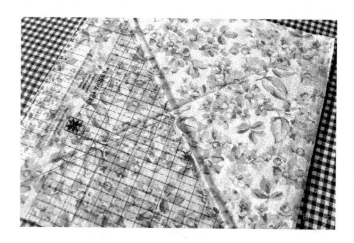

4. With your sewing machine and the walking foot attachment quilt along the stitching lines.

Sewing the quilt together

1. After quilting all your sandwiches, arrange the blocks in five rows of six squares alternating the design blocks and cotton print blocks.

2. Still using the walking foot attachment, stitch the blocks in each row together using a ½" seam allowance. Make sure you put the BACK SIDE of the quilt TOGETHER when joining the blocks. The seam allowance needs to end up on the FRONT of the quilt.

3. Then stitch each row together using a ½" seam allowance making sure you alternate the design blocks and cotton print blocks.

Note: When sewing the rows together it doesn't matter if you press the seams open or push them to one side because the join is disguised under the fluffiness of the seam allowance and you don't really notice which way the seams are going.

4. Stitch a ½" seam around the entire outside edge of the quilt for a "raggedy" border.

Finishing

1. Using rag quilt snips or a sharp pair of scissors, clip all the seam allowances at approximately ½" intervals. Clip close to the stitching lines, taking care not to cut through them.

2. Finish the quilt by washing in the washing machine to fray the exposed seams. Shake your quilt out to remove loose threads before putting your quilt in the dryer. Remember to wash in cold water with no harsh detergents and dry on a low setting. The more you wash and dry your quilt the fluffier it will become.

Envelope Pillow Covers

©Vicki Becker Photography

Quick and easy! Use any embroidey design you wish for these pillow covers. The flower design was enlarged to 190% and the flower wreath enlarged to 200%. The flower designs used for the pillows can be found on page 25 and 27.

Finished pillow size

16" x 16"

Material

3/4 yd medium weight 100% cotton solids. Unbleached muslin, broadcloth, and quilters cotton are all good choices.

1- 16" pillow form

Matching sewing thread

Cutting

1. Cut one 16½" square for the pillow front panel.

2. Cut two 16½" x 12" pieces for the pillow back.

Preparing the pillow front

Transfer the design of your choice to the pillow front panel. Color and heat set if desired. Outline and highlight each design with ink or embroidery.

Sewing

1. To prepare the back take the long outside edge of each back piece and fold over ½" of the fabric and press with your iron. Fold again by another ½" and press. Sew this hem close to the inside edge.

2. Lay the front pillow piece on a flat surface with the wrong side facing down, right side facing up. Align the back pieces on top of the front panel, right sides together.

Be sure the hemmed edges of the back pieces face in and the long raw side edges of the back pieces align with the side edges of the front panel. The back pieces will overlap in the center. Pin in place.

3. Sew a ¼" seam around the entire outer edges of the pillow cover.

4. Clip the corners and turn right side out. Use a blunt object such as a crochet hook to push the corners out.

Patchwork Pillow Covers

Pretty patchwork! Embellished with rick rack and buttons. Choose either a large or small center square for your cover. Embroider with redwork or any color your heart desires.

Finished pillow size

16" x 16"

Material (for one pillow cover)

½ yd medium weight cotton print fabric

¾ yd medium weight cotton solid fabric

1- 16" purchased pillow form

Matching sewing thread

Cutting - Front

Large Center Square Front Pillow Panel

1- 10½" x 10½" square from solid fabric

2- 10½" x 3½" print fabric strips

2- 16½" x 3½" print fabric strips

Small Center Square Front Pillow Panel

1- 8½" x 8½" square from solid fabric

2- 8½" x 4½" print fabric strips

2- 16½" x 4½" print fabric strips

Back

2. Cut two 16½" X 12" pieces from solid fabric for the pillow back.

Preparing the pillow front

Transfer the design of your choice to the pillow front center square. Color and heat set if desired. Outline and highlight each design with ink or embroidery.

Sewing

1. To sew the front pillow panels begin by sewing with a ¼" seam the short strips to each side of the square. Press the seams to one side. Next sew the long strips to the top and bottom of the square. Press the seams to one side. Top stitch rick rack to pillow front as desired.

2. To prepare the pillow back take the long outside edge of each back piece and fold over ½" of the fabric and press with your iron. Fold again by another ½" and press. Sew this hem close to the inside edge.

3. Lay the front pillow piece on a flat surface with the wrong side facing down, right side facing up. Align the back pieces on top of the front panel, right sides together.

Be sure the hemmed edges of the back pieces face in and the long raw side edges of the back pieces align with the side edges of the front panel. The back pieces will overlap in the center. Pin in place.

4. Sew a ¼" seam around the entire outer edges of the pillow cover.

5. Clip the corners and turn right side out. Use a blunt object such as a crochet hook to push corners out.

6. Embellish pillow cover with assorted decorative buttons as desired.

The Designs

The designs are in a line art style for hand embroidering and color tinting. You can embroider the designs all in one color as in red work or use a variety of colors and add color tinting with crayons if you wish.

There are 24 vintage designs in three sizes printed on one side of the page. You can enlarge or reduce the designs to fit your projects as needed. In addition to the 24 vintage designs you will also find other designs scattered amoung the pages of the book that can be traced and used for embroidery as well.

VINTAGE

HAND EMBROIDERY

PATTERNS

VINTAGE

HAND EMBROIDERY

PATTERNS

VINTAGE

HAND EMBROIDERY

PATTERNS

VINTAGE

HAND EMBROIDERY

PATTERNS

VINTAGE

HAND EMBROIDERY

PATTERNS

VINTAGE

HAND EMBROIDERY

PATTERNS

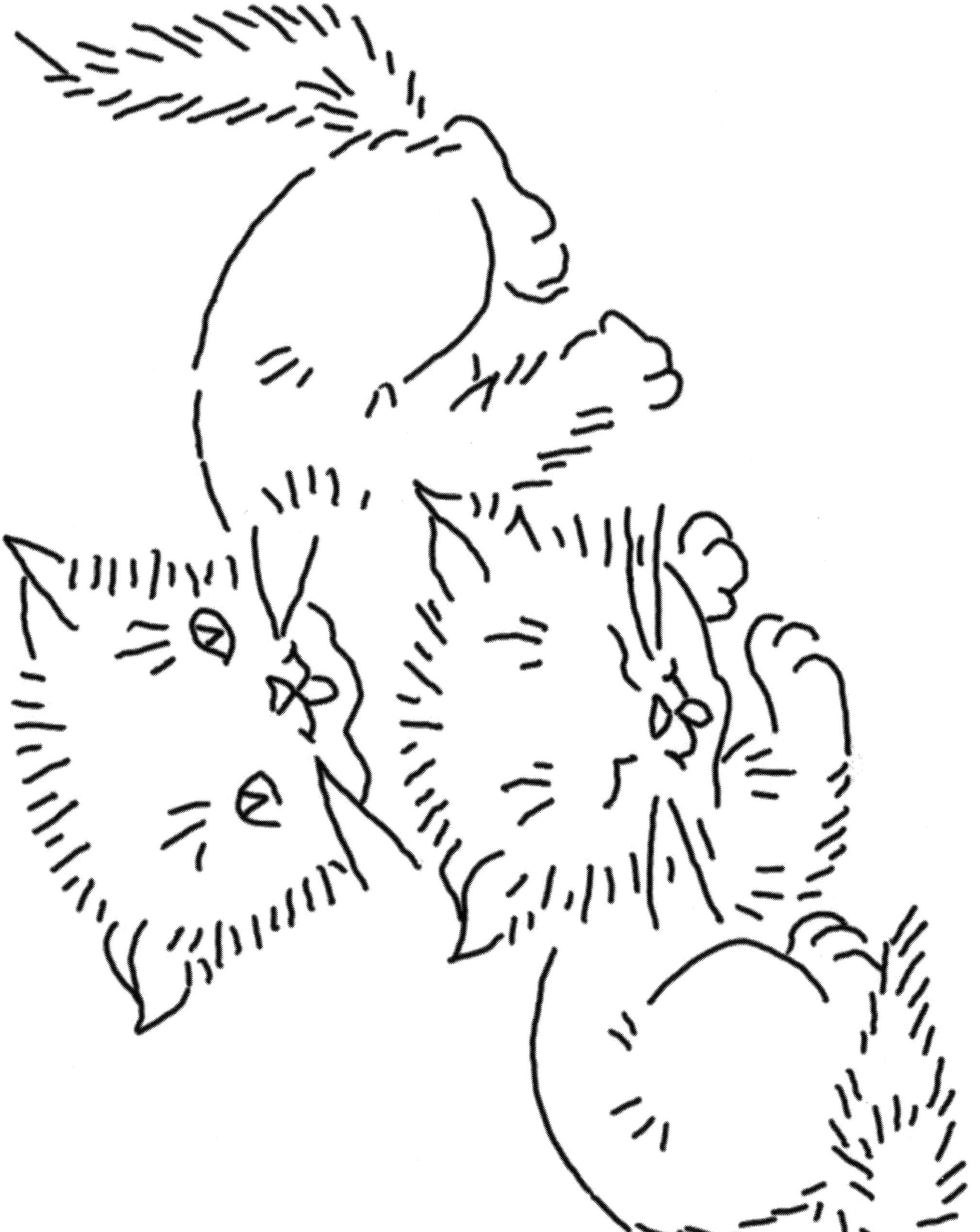

VINTAGE

HAND EMBROIDERY

PATTERNS

VINTAGE

HAND EMBROIDERY

PATTERNS

VINTAGE

HAND EMBROIDERY

PATTERNS

VINTAGE

HAND EMBROIDERY

PATTERNS

VINTAGE

HAND EMBROIDERY

PATTERNS

VINTAGE

HAND EMBROIDERY

PATTERNS

VINTAGE

HAND EMBROIDERY

PATTERNS

VINTAGE

HAND EMBROIDERY

PATTERNS

VINTAGE

HAND EMBROIDERY

PATTERNS

59

VINTAGE
HAND EMBROIDERY
PATTERNS

VINTAGE

HAND EMBROIDERY

PATTERNS

VINTAGE

HAND EMBROIDERY

PATTERNS

VINTAGE

HAND EMBROIDERY

PATTERNS

VINTAGE

HAND EMBROIDERY

PATTERNS

VINTAGE

HAND EMBROIDERY

PATTERNS

VINTAGE

HAND EMBROIDERY

PATTERNS

VINTAGE

HAND EMBROIDERY

PATTERNS

VINTAGE

HAND EMBROIDERY

PATTERNS

VINTAGE

HAND EMBROIDERY

PATTERNS

VINTAGE

HAND EMBROIDERY

PATTERNS

VINTAGE

HAND EMBROIDERY

PATTERNS

VINTAGE

HAND EMBROIDERY

PATTERNS

VINTAGE

HAND EMBROIDERY

PATTERNS

VINTAGE

HAND EMBROIDERY

PATTERNS

VINTAGE

HAND EMBROIDERY

PATTERNS

VINTAGE

HAND EMBROIDERY

PATTERNS

VINTAGE

HAND EMBROIDERY

PATTERNS

VINTAGE

HAND EMBROIDERY

PATTERNS

VINTAGE

HAND EMBROIDERY

PATTERNS

VINTAGE

HAND EMBROIDERY

PATTERNS

VINTAGE

HAND EMBROIDERY

PATTERNS

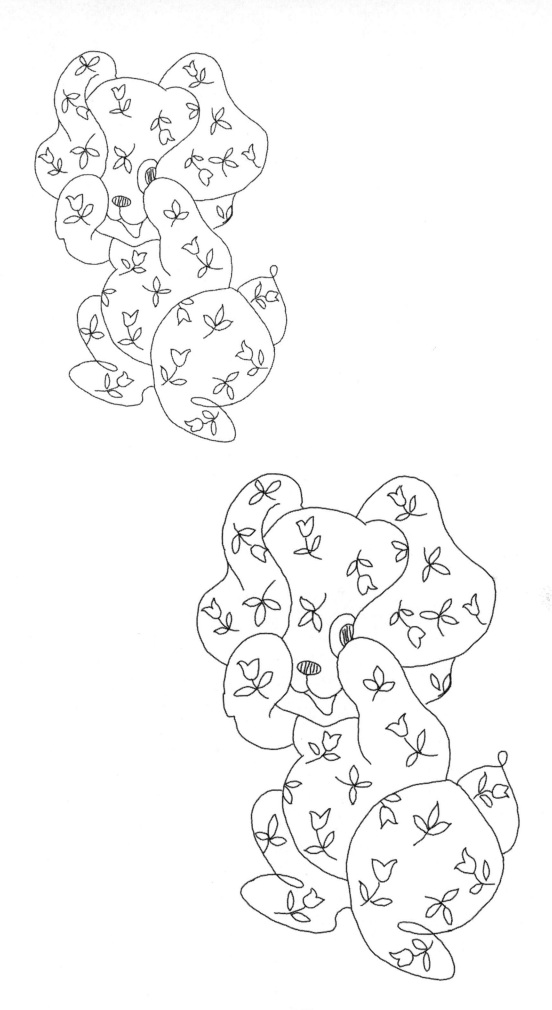

VINTAGE

HAND EMBROIDERY

PATTERNS

VINTAGE

HAND EMBROIDERY

PATTERNS

VINTAGE

HAND EMBROIDERY

PATTERNS

VINTAGE

HAND EMBROIDERY

PATTERNS

VINTAGE
HAND EMBROIDERY
PATTERNS

VINTAGE

HAND EMBROIDERY

PATTERNS

VINTAGE

HAND EMBROIDERY

PATTERNS

VINTAGE

HAND EMBROIDERY

PATTERNS

Made in the USA
Las Vegas, NV
26 November 2024

12684282R00070